STEINER'S
SIMPLE GRAMMAR GUIDE

*YES YOU CAN
SPEAK IT AND WRITE IT RIGHT*

Copyright Notice

Copyright laws protect this book. Reproduction of it in any form without permission from the copyright owner is prohibited.

Copyright © 2021 Sharon C. Steiner

INTRODUCTION

My mission is to enlighten and educate people via this guide. I hope this guide will assist people in speaking and writing and help them make the correct choice of words. I always had a strong interest in grammar and how certain words are spoken and written. I always wanted to put something together to show people the correct usage for words that I often see and hear misused or misspelled. I correct individuals close to me when I read something they wrote or heard something they said.

For many years, I procrastinated writing some type of English/grammar book. Finally, I began writing it and just went back to it several times but did nothing. I later decided to do something different, which was to put together a grammar guide. This guide includes words and meanings that I often see and hear in daily conversations, public interviews (seen on National TV), and business emails. Unfortunately, these words are misused and misspelled by professionals on all levels, college students, and others.

Using proper grammar has always been a passion for me, and this is why I wanted to put this guide together. It will educate you on how to speak it and write it right.

CONTENTS

Introduction 3

Frequently Misused Words 6

Subject-Verb Agreement 28

Singular-Plural Words 30

NOTE: Each word has a brief meaning and short sentence. Words can have different meanings; all meanings are not in this guide.

FREQUENTLY MISUSED WORDS

- A-use before a word beginning with a consonant (a book); or consonant sound (a university)

    She has a quiet personality.
    I will buy you a book.

- AN-use before a word beginning with a vowel (an apple/an onion/an example/or a vowel sound (an honor/an hour)

    Len is an excellent student.
    Joy is an honor student.
    I was nominated for an Oscar award.
    I was scheduled to get an x-ray.

- ACCEPT-to take or receive something

    Sharon will accept your dinner invitation.
    I accept all major credit cards.

    EXCEPT-to leave out or exclude

    We're all going except John.
    No one except Val knew the answer.

Everyone except Bea had a ticket for the show.

- ACCESS-able to enter

    The plumber did not have access to the pipes.

    ASSESS–to determine the amount or rate of something
    The insurance adjuster will assess the damages to my car.

- ADDITION-something or someone added
    The baby is a new addition to our family.

    EDITION-the form in which something is produced
    I bought the hardback edition of the book.

- ADVICE-an opinion
    I gave you my advice.

    ADVISE-to give a recommendation
    I advised you not to go.

- AFFECT-to influence
    The play positively affected me.

EFFECT-result/to accomplish
The law will go into effect next month.

- ALL READY-completely prepared/all are ready
  The students were all ready to take the test.

  ALREADY-before now
  The teacher was already at school.

- ALL TOGETHER-everyone or everything together
  We were all together at the ceremony.

  ALTOGETHER-totally/completely
  Altogether, fifty people were injured on the boat.

- ALL WAYS-different ways of getting the same result
  They tried all ways to put out the fire.

  ALWAYS-continuously/forever
  I always wanted to write this book.
  I will always love you.

- ALTAR-SACRED SPACE
  Place the cross on the altar.

  ALTER-tailor/to change
  The seamstress will alter my dress.

- ANGEL-a spiritual being/kind and loveable person
  An angel is watching over me.

  ANGLE-the space between two intersecting lines
  The lot only has angle spaces available.

- A PART-to join
  I want to be a part of the show.

  APART-to separate
  The brick wall kept us apart.

- APPRAISE-assess the value
  The house was appraised for $200,000.

  APPRISE-to inform
  I will apprise her of my resignation.

- ASSURE-give confidence to

I assure you we will not be late.

ENSURE-make sure/guarantee
Please ensure the accuracy of the document.

INSURE-take out insurance
Liberty Mutual will insure my car.

➢ BARE-least possible
The walls in my house are bare.

BEAR-to tolerate
I can't bear the pain.

➢ BOUGHT-to buy something
Joe bought his mother a new car.

BROUGHT-past tense of bring
Joe brought the car home when she was asleep.

➢ BREATH-intake of air
Take a deep breath and relax.

BREATHE-to inhale and exhale
He could not breathe on his own.

- CAPITAL-city/money
  Washington DC is the nation's capital.

  I don't have enough capital to move on with my project.

  CAPITOL-a building
  The Capitol is the building where Congress meets.

- CITE-to quote
  I cited what I read about the virus.

  SIGHT-ability to see
  My sight is improving in both eyes.

  SITE-a place/location
  I'm looking for a site to build a school.

- COMPLEMENT-to enhance/improve
  White trimming can complement the gray walls.

  COMPLIMENT-to praise/flatter
  I always compliment her new hairstyles.

- CONFIDANT-someone to trust with secrets
  He's my closest confidant.

CONFIDENT-being certain of something
I am confident about winning the part for the play.

➢ CONSCIENCE-sense of right and wrong
A clear conscience helps you make the right choices.

CONSCIOUS-awareness of oneself
The victim was conscious and talking.

➢ COUNCIL-an elected group that governs or leads
Washington, DC has thirteen council members.

COUNSEL-to give advice
The teacher counseled the student.

➢ DEVICE-type of tool/gadget
I used the device to repair the chair.

DEVISE-to work out or create something
The staff will devise a plan to build a shed.

➢ DO-to do something

He will do his work early.

DUE-to owe something
The assignment is due today.

DEW-water droplet
There was dew on the cars.

➢ FAZE-bothered/upset
The loud noise didn't faze him.

PHASE-to do something over a period of time
The next phase of my project will begin next month.

➢ FISCAL-relating to money
The Federal Government's fiscal year ends September 30th.

PHYSICAL-relating to the body
My physical exam is scheduled for next week.

➢ HALL-large room or passageway
The dance will be at Treasury Hall.

HAUL-to move
The workers will haul away the debris.

➤ HUMAN-a person
The human brain is very delicate.

HUMANE-showing compassion and kindness
It's not humane to kill someone.

➤ IDLE-pass time doing nothing
She's been idle for a long time.

IDOL-person highly adored
I'm an idol to the people in my community.

➤ INSTANCE-occurrence/example
This report is an instance of good work.

INSTANTS-very brief period
The noise only lasted a few instants.

➤ KNOW-to have knowledge
I will get to know him soon.

NO-not at all/not so
No, you cannot go.

- LATER-at a later time
  I'll see you later today.

  LATTER-the second of two things or people mentioned
  They like the latter of the two.

- LOOSE-not tight
  My hat was loose on my head.

  LOSE-misplace or defeated
  Did she lose her bag?

  LOSS-to lose someone or something
  I'm sorry for the loss of your cat.

  LOST-cannot find
  I lost my new camera.

- MALL-a place to shop
  The mall is being renovated and expanded.

  MAUL-to injure roughly
  A large dog mauled Dave.

- MORAL-sense of right and wrong
  People have different moral standards.

MORALE-mental/emotional condition
The morale at work is very low.

➤ PASSED-to pass
Last month passed fast.

PAST-no longer exist
Don't dwell on the past.

➤ PATIENCE-to accept delay
They don't have the patience to do the job.

PATIENTS-people receiving medical care
Two patients shared a room in the hospital.

➤ PERSONAL-refers to a person
This is a personal matter.

PERSONNEL-a department responsible for employee matters
Personnel will begin processing my retirement papers.

➤ PRECEDE-go or come before
She was preceded in death by her brother.

PROCEED-move forward
I will proceed with the purchase.

➤ PRESENCE-being present
I enjoyed his presence at the show.

PRESENTS-to give gifts
I gave birthday presents to the children.

➤ PRINCIPAL-someone in charge
My friend is the principal of an elementary school.

PRINCIPLE-basic truth
She's a woman of principle.

➤ SAIL-travel on water
The boat will sail at noon today.

SALE-to sell something
The car is on sale at a reasonable price.

SELL-to give up something for money
I'm going to sell my products at a flea market.

CELL-phone/building blocks of all living things
We all know what a cell phone is.

There are three types of blood cells in the human body.

➢ STATIONARY-not moving/still
I bought a stationary bike to exercise.

STATIONERY-writing paper
The stationery came in a variety of colors.

➢ SUPPOSE-to think or guess
I suppose I'll be going.

SUPPOSED TO-expected to do something
I'm supposed to work today.

➢ THAN-comparisons
Kay is taller than her brother.

THEN-indicates time
I was a student back then.

➢ THEIR-belonging to them
Do you have their records?

THEY'RE-contraction for they are
They're going on an extended vacation next year.

THERE-at that place/opposite of here/to begin a sentence
There are five movie theaters in town.

➤ THREW-past tense of throw
Tim threw a rock and broke a window.

THROUGH-from one end to another/finished
We rode our bikes through the park.

THRU-slang for through
We danced thru the night.

➤ TO-movement toward a person or place
I'll be going to the library later today.

TOO-also/more than enough
I love you too.
We arrived too late for the event.

TWO-the number 2
Only two of the girls will be competing.

- USE-something that was done in the past
  I use to smoke.

  USED TO-action or habit in the past/something routine or familiar

  I used to jump rope every day.

- VIAL-small plastic or glass container
  Vaccines are stored in vials.

  VILE-unpleasant/very offensive
  The car has a vile smell.

- WEAR-to have on the body
  I'll wear a light jacket today.

  WHERE-refers to a place
  Where are the children going to play?

- WE'RE-contraction for we are
  We're both aware of what happened.

  WERE-past tense
  The trays were in a stack.

- WHOSE-possessive of who
  Whose papers are these?

  WHO'S-contraction for who is
  Who's the one wearing the black jacket?

- YOUR-belonging to you
  Is that your book on the table?

  YOU'RE-contraction for you are
  You're welcome. (NOT YOUR WELCOME)
  You're the one. (NOT YOUR THE ONE)

  YOURS-possessive of you
  This is yours.
  It's all yours.

THE WORD "OF" SHOULD NEVER BE USED AS A HELPING VERB.

When we speak, we hear the "of" sound and think it's of, but the correct word to use is have. Using contractions keep the speech flowing.

INCORRECT: Could of/Should of/Would of/May of/Might of
CORRECT: Could have/Should have/Would have
Could've/Should've/Would've – these are contractions we use speaking when combining two words.

The contractions Should've/Could've/Would've can also be used below

INCORRECT: Should of ate
CORRECT: Should have eaten

INCORRECT: Could of ate
CORRECT: Could have eaten

INCORRECT: Should of blew
CORRECT: Should have blown

INCORRECT: Could of blew
CORRECT: Could have blown

INCORRECT: Should of chose
CORRECT: Should have chosen

INCORRECT: Could of chose
CORRECT: Could have chosen

INCORRECT: Should of did
CORRECT: Should have done

INCORRECT: Could of did
CORRECT: Could have done

INCORRECT: Should of drove
CORRECT: Should have driven

INCORRECT: Could of drove
CORRECT: Could have driven

INCORRECT: Should of fell
CORRECT: Should have fallen

INCORRECT: Could of fell
CORRECT: Could have fallen

INCORRECT: Should of flew
CORRECT: Should have flown

INCORRECT: Could of flew
CORRECT: Could have flown

INCORRECT: Should of got
CORRECT: Should have gotten

INCORRECT: Could of got
CORRECT: Could have gotten

INCORRECT: Should of knew
CORRECT: Should have known

INCORRECT: Could of knew
CORRECT: Could have known

INCORRECT: Should of saw
CORRECT: Should have seen

INCORRECT: Could of saw
CORRECT: Could have seen

INCORRECT: Should of spoke
CORRECT: Should have spoken

INCORRECT: Could of spoke
CORRECT: Could have spoken

INCORRECT: Should of threw
CORRECT: Should have thrown

INCORRECT: Could of threw
CORRECT: Could have thrown

INCORRECT: Should of took
CORRECT: Should have taken

INCORRECT: Could of took
CORRECT: Could have taken

INCORRECT: Should of went
CORRECT: Should have gone

INCORRECT: Could of went
CORRECT: Could have gone

INCORRECT: Should of wore
CORRECT: Should have worn

INCORRECT: Could of wore
CORRECT: Could have worn

INCORRECT: Should of wrote
CORRECT: Should have written

INCORRECT: Could of wrote
CORRECT: Could have written

MAY HAVE/MIGHT HAVE:
I may have (or may've) dropped my keys outside.
I might have (or might've) dropped my keys outside.

MAY (likely) MIGHT (unlikely)
I may start looking for a new car.
I might start looking for a new car.

MAY can also be used to ask for and give permission or express a wish

May I borrow your car?
You may borrow my car.
May you have a wonderful day.

SEEN (frequently misused)

A helping verb is always used before the word seen.
(e.g., she has seen, they've seen, I've never seen, have you seen, may have seen)

INCORRECT: I seen, we seen, they seen
CORRECT: I've seen, we've seen, they've seen
        I saw, we saw, they saw

SUBJECT-VERB AGREEMENT

Subjects and verbs must agree. If the subject is singular, the verb must be singular. If the subject is plural, the verb must be plural. When the subject is a name, he, she or it, add an "s" or "es" to the verb.

The books are on the shelf. (plural)
The book is on the shelf. (singular)

My bags are heavy. (plural)
My bag is heavy. (singular)

Tim and Mary are friends. (plural)
Tim is my friend. (Singular)

He wants you to go with us. (singular)
They want you to go with us. (plural)

My class schedules are ready. (plural)
My class schedule is ready. (singular)

Some pronouns can be singular or plural, depending on how you use them.

It snows every year in DC.
It was nice meeting you.
It's hard to believe.
It works fine.
It will be summer soon.
I have a new plan.

SINGULAR-PLURAL WORDS

Words that are both singular and plural
(*frequently misused with an "s" on the end)

Deer*
Dice*
Information
Moose
Music
News
Reindeer*
Scissors
Series
Sheep*
Shrimp*
Species
Trousers

I carefully chose the words in this guide, hoping that it'll bring awareness to them. They're often misused and confused.

I believe self-teaching is an important aspect of one's life. Don't think you're too old or young to learn something new or brush up on your skills. No matter where you're in life, there's always something to learn, whether it's big or small.

Write the vision and make it clear so that it can be read easily and quickly.   Habakkuk 2

www.ingramcontent.com/pod-product-compliance
Lightning Source LLC
Chambersburg PA
CBHW031207160426
43193CB00008B/540